The Sprinkling of The Blood

The Sprinkling of The Blood

◆

Releasing the Power of the Blood of Jesus to Work in Your Life

"By faith he kept the Passover and the sprinkling of blood, lest he who destroyed the firstborn should touch them." Hebrews 11:28

Winston Farmer

iUniverse, Inc.
New York Lincoln Shanghai

The Sprinkling of The Blood
Releasing the Power of the Blood of Jesus to Work in Your Life

Copyright © 2006 by WINSTON FARMER

All rights reserved. No part of this book may be used or reproduced by any means, graphic, electronic, or mechanical, including photocopying, recording, taping or by any information storage retrieval system without the written permission of the publisher except in the case of brief quotations embodied in critical articles and reviews.

iUniverse books may be ordered through booksellers or by contacting:

iUniverse
2021 Pine Lake Road, Suite 100
Lincoln, NE 68512
www.iuniverse.com
1-800-Authors (1-800-288-4677)

The views expressed in this work are solely those of the author and do not necessarily reflect the views of the publisher, and the publisher hereby disclaims any responsibility for them.

ISBN-13: 978-0-595-41486-4 (pbk)
ISBN-13: 978-0-595-85835-4 (ebk)
ISBN-10: 0-595-41486-9 (pbk)
ISBN-10: 0-595-85835-X (ebk)

Printed in the United States of America

Unless otherwise indicated, all Scripture quotations are taken from the New King James Version. Copyright © 1982 by Thomas Nelson, Inc. Used by permission. All rights reserved.

Scripture quotations marked **AMP** are taken from the Amplified® Bible, Copyright © 1954, 1958, 1962, 1964, 1965, 1987 by The Lockman Foundation Used by permission

Scripture quotations marked **NIV** are taken from HOLY BIBLE, NEW INTERNATIONAL VERSION ® Copyright © 1973, 1978, 1984 by International Bible Society

Scripture quotations marked **NASB** are taken from the NEW AMERICAN STANDARD BIBLE®, Copyright © 1960, 1962, 1963, 1968, 1971, 1972, 1973, 1975, 1977, 1995 by The Lockman Foundation. Used by permission.

Scripture quotations marked **THE MESSAGE** are taken from *The Message* by Eugene H. Peterson, copyright (c) 1993, 1994, 1995, 1996, 2000, 2001, 2002. Used by permission of NavPress Publishing Group. All rights reserved.

Scripture quotations marked **NLT** are taken from the Holy Bible, New Living Translation, copyright 1996. Used by permission of Tyndale House Publishers, Inc., Wheaton, Illinois 60189. All rights reserved.
Table of Contents

Contents

Chapter 1	The Power in the Speaking Blood 1
Chapter 2	Knowledge is Power. 7
Chapter 3	Why You Must Have Faith in The Blood 13
Chapter 4	Life Is In The Blood 22
Chapter 5	Application of The Blood 31
Chapter 6	"No Fear" Through The Blood 48
Chapter 7	Healed By The Blood 55
Chapter 8	Abundance Through The Blood 62
Chapter 9	The Sprinkling of The Blood. 72

Applying the Blood of Jesus for Your Salvation 81

1

The Power in the Speaking Blood

My First "Pleading the Blood" Experience

Several years ago my wife told me about an experience she had at a church we were attending. It was an experience that would change my view of the blood of Jesus forever. She had volunteered to work in the children's church.

In order to work with the children, it was required that she first observes some classes. The first week she had observed a class that was wild and unruly. It seemed the teacher had a hard time controlling the children. My wife wasn't sure if she really wanted to teach in that environment. There was very little order in this class and they didn't get much accomplished.

She went back the next week and observed the same class. The class was totally different. The children were the same but there was a different teacher. She couldn't help but notice a stark contrast between this class and the one she observed a week earlier. The children were well behaved and respectful. There was a peace over the classroom that had been absent the week before.

The teacher didn't seem to do anything differently. The children were the same ones that had been there the week before. My wife talked to the teacher after the class. She commented on how she had observed a marked difference in the behavior and atmosphere in the class from the week before. The teacher responded, *"That's because I plead the blood of Jesus over the class. Before class starts I walk around the room pleading the blood over every corner".*

When my wife old me this story, something grabbed me inside. I had to find out more about this "pleading the blood" stuff. You see, as a salesman I'm interested in anything that brings positive results. I've seen that just by tweaking a sales message you can produce a dramatic increase in sales.

I'd been confessing the word of God for years with some measure of results. Everyday I would say what the bible says about me. Proverbs 18:21 says that death and life are in the power of the tongue. But I'd never "pled the blood of Jesus" as this woman had done. I heard about this but I never had any teaching on the subject. I was impressed with the tangible and immediate results my wife had witnessed. I began to think that there was something missing in my prayers and confessions. I wanted to find out more about the power of the blood of Jesus.

A Search For Knowledge

I started to look for any books or tapes that I could find on the subject of the blood of Jesus. I was surprised that there weren't many books on the subject, even in Christian bookstores. It seemed strange that with so many Christian books published today, a topic as important as the blood of Jesus seemed to be in short supply. But every time I've been hungry to find out something about God's word, God has given me answers. He is the rewarder of them that diligently seek Him (Heb.11.6).

I did locate a few books that helped me but I also began to seek God for a revelation of the power of confessing the blood of Jesus. Why do we need to speak or "plead" the blood out loud? Is this scriptural or something man made and passed down as gospel.

I found some answers that I will share in this book. Let me say first that you don't need to plead the blood of Jesus everyday to stay saved. This doesn't improve your position in heaven. Your inheritance is secure, incorruptible and undefiled and reserved for you in heaven (1 Peter 1:3). This is true for all who have received Jesus Christ as Lord and Savior.

However, speaking or pleading the blood of Jesus will improve the quality of your life here on earth. It's a powerful weapon that God has given us to enforce the devil's defeat. The blood of Jesus never fails when it is applied by faith. This is the key. It must be applied by faith. You may have pled the blood in your prayer life before. Maybe you heard or read about someone who pled the blood of Jesus and experience victory in his or her life. You said, "I think I'll try that". You tried it and it didn't work.

That's the problem. You "tried" the blood of Jesus with no faith in it. Faith in the blood is required and faith comes by hearing the word of God (Romans 5:17). You must plead the blood with total confidence in its power to deliver you from any situation your adversary, the devil, tries to bring against you or your family.

The Sprinkled Blood

Let me just say that there is nothing in the bible that says we are to "plead" the blood of Jesus. I've never found those words in the Old or New Testament. However, the bible does tell us that the Old Testament or Covenant is given to us as an example that we can use in our walk as New Testament believers.

1 Cor 10:1-6
10:1 For I do not want you to be ignorant of the fact, brothers, that our forefathers were all under the cloud and that they all passed through the sea. 2 They were all baptized into Moses in the cloud and in the sea. 3 They all ate the same spiritual food 4 and drank the same spiritual drink; for they drank from the spiritual rock that accompanied them, and that rock was Christ. 5 Nevertheless, God was not pleased with most of them; their bodies were scattered over the desert.

6 Now these things occurred as examples to keep us from setting our hearts on evil things as they did. NIV

We are to read the Old Testament as an example. The God of Abraham, Isaac and Jacob is our Father God. He is the same God and doesn't change. He deals with His covenant children the same way. We just have a better covenant established on better promises (Heb.8.6).

What is our example for pleading the blood of Jesus? I would not dare say that I know every one of them contained in the Old Testament. I do not have a revelation of the entire word of God. No one does except Jesus. But we can take a look at a very powerful example of redemption through blood. It's the story of the Passover. Even if you're familiar with the story, please stop and read Exodus 12.

Hebrews 11:28 says, *"by faith he (Moses) kept the Passover and the sprinkling of blood, lest he who destroyed the firstborn should touch them".*
The Passover is our example of applying the blood of Jesus for deliverance and protection from the destroyer. The children of Israel applied the blood of the Passover lamb to their homes by faith. They knew nothing else but that God had commanded Moses to command them to take this action.

It took faith to apply that blood, just like it takes faith today to apply the blood of Jesus. I'm convinced that pride will not let many Christians experience the power of the blood of Christ in everyday life. Why? Because it sounds too simple. Many would rather work hard in their own might rather than trust in the resurrection power of the blood. They feel that if they don't work up a sweat and pray for hours about something, they haven't really prayed.

There's nothing wrong with praying for hours if you're praying the right way. Many hours of prayer and pleading with God could be eliminated with the simple acknowledgement and trust in the finished work of the blood of the cross. This prayer time could be spent praising and thanking

God for what His blood has already accomplished for us. This is what pleases our Heavenly Father.

In the first Passover, the head of the household physically applied the blood of the lamb to the doorpost. Everything Israel did in the flesh, the Christian does by faith. Hebrews 11:28 says that Moses "sprinkled" the blood by faith. We can sprinkle the blood of Christ, our Passover, by faith. Faith is released when you speak it out of your mouth. We'll get into this more in depth in Chapter 3, "Why You Must Have Faith in The Blood".

A Prayer Life of Power

There is a new dimension of prayer power that awaits you. That power is in the life of God Himself. That power is the same power that raised Jesus from the dead (Hebrews 13:20). That power is in His blood because the life of all flesh is in the blood (Lev.17.11). Jesus blood contains the life of God. It is holy, incorruptible blood that is still alive in heaven right now (Heb.12.24).

When you speak the blood of Jesus in your prayers, you release all of God's life and power that delivered you from the authority of the devil when you made Jesus the Lord of your life.

Colossians 1:13-14
13 He has delivered us from the power of darkness and conveyed us into the kingdom of the Son of His love, 14 in whom we have redemption through His blood, the forgiveness of sins.

The blood of Jesus has given us a new life in God. We are new creatures in Christ (2 Corinthians 5:17). We have a new spiritual DNA through the incorruptible and precious blood of Christ (1Peter 1:18).

Nothing can stop the power of the blood of Jesus when spoken in faith. It's a spiritual weapon that is underused by many believers. But before you can use the blood of Jesus as a spiritual weapon, you need knowledge of what the blood has done for you. Hosea 4:6 says God's people are destroyed for lack of knowledge.

Knowledge plus confidence produces faith. My prayer is that this book will give you more knowledge of the power of the blood of Jesus. Throughout the book, the words "pleading", "sprinkling" or "applying" the blood are used. All three refer to speaking the blood in faith. No matter what term you prefer to use, the results will be the same. A confident and fruitful prayer life based on the living, redeeming blood of Jesus Christ!

2

Knowledge is Power

2 Peter 1:2-3
2 Grace and peace be multiplied to you in the knowledge of God and of Jesus our Lord, 3 as His divine power has given to us all things that pertain to life and godliness, through the knowledge of Him who called us by glory and virtue

Hebrews 10:38 says that "the just shall live by faith". Faith needs an object. If you say, "I have faith" or "I'm living by my faith", you must have faith *in something*.

To say you are living by faith is meaningless unless you can point to the object of that faith. What do you have faith in? Many Christians would answer, "the word of God" or God himself. That had always been my response. But I've learned that we must have a more specific object of our faith. To say you have faith in God only means something if you know what God has done *and* will do for you.

The Blood as an Object for Faith

The shedding of Jesus' blood is the most powerful thing God ever did for the world. It *is* the love of God in action. John 3:16 is a foundational scripture that millions have based their eternal salvation on.

John 3:16
For God so loved the world that He *gave* His only begotten Son, that whoever believes in Him should not perish but have everlasting life.

God "gave" Jesus through the act of shedding His blood. To "believe in Him" does not mean to merely believe that He existed. There are many who have believed that Jesus once lived and walked the earth, but refuse to accept Him as their Savior. Sad to say, they will die in their sins (John 8:24).

When you believe His blood was shed for you and accept the fact that you need His blood sacrifice to remit you of your sins, you receive the benefits of the blood sacrifice. You become a born-again child of God.

But for many Christians, that's the last time the blood was applied or sprinkled on their lives. The blood of Jesus was powerful enough to remit all of our sins, deliver us from the authority of the devil and make us new creatures. Why would we ignore it's power for the balance of our lives here on earth? Many believers never mention the blood in their prayer life or confessions.

Why is the blood of Jesus given such little honor? I believe it's because of a lack of knowledge. I also believe it's because of a lack of interest. Blood is not a civilized subject. That's a problem with many Christians today. They're too civilized and the blood is a messy subject. It's okay to sing about it in church once in a while, but don't bring it into everyday conversation. That's foolish. That kind of attitude will make the blood powerless in your life. You have to honor the blood of Jesus and give it the proper position in your thinking and speaking. We can't ignore what the word of God instructs us to do. It says **we are to have faith in the blood of Jesus**. This truth is found in Galatians 2:20.

Gal 2:20
I have been crucified with Christ; it is no longer I who live, but Christ lives in me; and the life which I now live in the flesh I live by faith in the Son of God, who loved me and gave Himself for me.

Notice the phrase "gave Himself for me". How did Jesus give Himself for us? He shed His blood. In fact, I want you to start reading the bible differently. Every time you read that Jesus gave Himself or died, replace that with *"shed His blood"*. Anytime the bible talks about Jesus death, it's talking about His shed blood. The death of Jesus would be of no consequence if He had not shed His blood. His life was not taken from Him (John 10:18). He gave it willingly and that life was contained in His blood. It was the blood that had the power to give you and I the life of God. He "gave Himself" by giving up His life, and that life was in His blood.

Leviticus 17:11
For the life of the flesh is in the blood, and I have given it to you upon the altar to make atonement for your souls; for it is the blood that makes atonement for the soul.'

Since the life of the flesh is in the blood and Jesus gave His life for us, we are to have faith in the Son of God and His blood that was shed for us. To have faith in the blood is to put our total trust in that blood to meet every need in our lives. In 2 Corinthians 1:9, the apostle Paul stated that he trusted not in himself but in God who raised the dead. I like the Message translation of this verse. It reads:

2 Cor 1:9
We felt like we'd been sent to death row, that it was all over for us. As it turned out, it was the best thing that could have happened. Instead of trusting in our own strength or wits to get out of it, we were forced to trust God totally—not a bad idea since he's the God who raises the dead!
THE MESSAGE

Think about that. Who would you rather trust? God, who raises the dead or yourself, who can't? It's really foolish to trust in yourself. After all, what have you really done in your own power? Oh you may have some natural accomplishments under your belt, but you couldn't do one of them without breathing. You can't make yourself breath, can you? Therefore, nothing you've accomplished is apart from God because He gave you the breath of life.

So it makes sense to trust in someone who can raise the dead rather than yourself. How did God raise Jesus from the dead? Hebrews tells us it was by His blood.

Hebrews 13:20-21
Now may the God of peace who brought up our Lord Jesus from the dead, that great Shepherd of the sheep, *through the blood of the everlasting covenant,* **21 make you complete in every good work to do His will, working in you what is well pleasing in His sight, through Jesus Christ, to whom be glory forever and ever. Amen.**

Everything we believe in Christianity is based on Jesus shedding His blood for us. There is no church without the blood. There is no new birth without the blood. There is no covenant without the blood. The more understanding we have of the blood and what it has purchased, the more faith we will have in it. You know the saying "knowledge is power". Well, the bible actually teaches this in the first chapter of 2nd Peter.

2 Peter 1:2-3
2 Grace and peace be multiplied to you in the knowledge of God and of Jesus our Lord, 3 as His divine power has given to us all things that pertain to life and godliness, *through the knowledge* **of Him who called us by glory and virtue,**

Let's look at the definitions of some of the words in 2 Peter 1:2. The word translated "grace" is defined by Thayer's Greek Lexicon as "goodwill, loving-kindness and favor". The word translated "peace" is the Greek word "eireenee". It is the Greek equivalent for the Hebrew word "shaalown". It means "security, safety and prosperity" or "wholeness". The word translated "knowledge" means to "become fully acquainted with". The word translated "multiply" simply means to increase.

With these definitions in mind, this scripture says that God's divine favor and wholeness are increased in our lives in proportion to the knowledge we have of God's word. I like to say, it this way; "favor and prosperity are increased in my life through the revealed knowledge of God's word". This scripture also says that God's divine power gives us all things that pertain to life and godliness *through the knowledge of God*. If that doesn't motivate you to spend more time studying your bible, I don't know what will!

A Purchased Inheritance

Knowledge of God's word is important. 3 John 1:2 says that we will "prosper and be in good health, just as our soul prospers". Another translation for the word soul is "mind". Too many Christians don't spend any time in God's word and therefore have no knowledge of it. And you can't receive or apply something you have no knowledge of. Some distant relative could have left you a million dollar inheritance, but if you have no knowledge of it you won't enjoy the money. It's there in an account. The trustees are waiting for you to come and claim it. But without your knowledge of this inheritance, it will just sit there not benefiting anyone.

God has given us an inheritance. It comes through His word.

Acts 20:32
"So now, brethren, I commend you to God and to the word of His grace, which is able to build you up and give you an inheritance among all those who are sanctified.

1 Peter 1:3-4 says that we have obtained an incorruptible inheritance through the resurrection of Jesus from the dead. The blood of Jesus purchased that inheritance and we need to have knowledge of that blood. Everything Jesus did for us on the cross can be increased in our lives

through revelation knowledge of the blood. I believe that as you read and meditate on the truths revealed in this book, the blood of Jesus will come alive to you. It will cease being just an historical fact, and begin to bless every area of your life ... the life God sent Jesus to give you in abundance!

John 10:10
10 The thief comes only in order to steal and kill and destroy. I came that they may have and enjoy life, and have it in abundance (to the full, till it overflows).
AMP

3

Why You Must Have Faith in The Blood

If you asked ten people on the street "what is faith?" you'll likely get ten different answers. People have come to use the word "faith" in our society so loosely that even many Christians don't have a biblical perspective on what faith is. This is evident in some of the criticism many "word of faith" preachers and churches receive today. "Oh, you're one of those faith people" some say, as if there was something wrong with that.

Well, the apostle Paul wrote, "the just shall live by faith" (Heb 10:31). The eleventh chapter of the book of Hebrews tells us that "without faith it is impossible to please God". It seems to me that these statements, made by the man who wrote two-thirds of the new testament, are so clear and direct that every believer would make it their top priority in life to find out what faith is and how to live by it. This book is about the blood of Jesus and specifically sprinkling or "pleading" the blood. In order for you to consistently plead the blood, you must have a working knowledge of the faith of God.

A Speaking Faith

The God kind of faith is a speaking faith. Throughout his walk on earth, Jesus used the authority of His spoken words to cast out demons, heal the sick, raise the dead, cause material increase and control the weather. He did this all through words. He must have walked by faith because He pleased God and that's impossible to do without faith.

Matthew 3:17
And suddenly a voice came from heaven, saying,"This is My beloved Son, *in whom I am well pleased.*"

Hebrews 11:6
But *without faith it is impossible to please Him,* for he who comes to God must believe that He is, and that He is a rewarder of those who diligently seek Him.

Jesus told his disciples to have the faith of God by speaking words and believing they would come to pass.

Mark 11:22-23
So Jesus answered and said to them, "Have faith in God.(or have the God kind of faith) 23 For assuredly, I say to you, whoever says to this mountain, 'Be removed and be cast into the sea,' and does not doubt in his heart, but believes that those things he says will be done, he will have whatever he says.
NKJV

The apostle Paul wrote about the spirit or the "attitude" of faith in 2 Corinthians.

2 Corinthians 4:13
And since we have the same spirit of faith, according to what is written, "I believed and therefore I spoke," we also believe and therefore speak,

Notice that the spirit of faith is believing *and* speaking. When you speak about something you believe, you are acting in faith. In fact you can't separate your words from what you believe. God made you that way. He constructed our bodies in a unique way. Because of where our tongue is located in our bodies, everything we say impacts what we believe. There is a direct connection between our tongue and our inner man.

James 3:3-6
Indeed, we put bits in horses' mouths that they may obey us, and we turn their whole body. 4 Look also at ships: although they are so large and are driven by fierce winds, they are turned by a very small rudder wherever the pilot desires. 5 Even so the tongue is a little member and boasts great things.
See how great a forest a little fire kindles! 6 And the tongue is a fire, a world of iniquity. *The tongue is so set among our members* **that it defiles the whole body, and sets on fire the course of nature; and it is set on fire by hell.**

James compares our tongues with the bits in a horse's mouth and the rudder on a ship. The comparison is that these small, otherwise insignificant parts control a large body. The placement of these parts in the ship and the horse gives them power to control these large bodies.

He goes on to say "*the tongue is so set among our members*". He's comparing the tongue in our mouths to the rudder and bit. In other words the tongue is a small part of your body and God placed it where it would control the entire body. The words you speak go directly into your inner man, the human spirit, and creates an imprint. The more you speak about something, the stronger that imprint gets until it's clear and you believe what you say. Not only do you speak what you believe, you also have the ability to change what you believe by what you choose to speak.

Speaking by Faith

The apostle Paul wrote, "the just shall live by faith". Living by faith is not an option for the believer. It is a commandment from God. You live by faith the same way you got saved—with words.

Romans 10:6-9
But the righteousness of faith speaks in this way, "Do not say in your heart, 'Who will ascend into heaven?'" (that is, to bring Christ down from above) 7 or, "'Who will descend into the abyss?'" (that is, to bring Christ up from the dead). 8 But what does it say? "The word is near you, in your mouth and in your heart" (that is, the word of faith which we preach): 9 that if you confess with your mouth the Lord Jesus and believe in your heart that God has raised Him from the dead, you will be saved.

If you're saved you got that way by believing that God raised Jesus from the dead for you *and* confessing with your mouth Jesus as Lord over your life. No one gets saved without a confession out of his or her mouth. Faith is not a silent thing. Someone might say, "I have faith in my heart". Well if that's true, it will be evident by what comes out of your mouth. You can't help that. Jesus said it this way:

Matthew 12:34
34 Brood of vipers! How can you, being evil, speak good things? For out of the abundance of the heart the mouth speaks.

You will speak whatever's in your heart. A good way to tell what you really believe is how you talk when you're under pressure. You may think you trust God and His word but the real test is how you talk when you don't have time to think.

What happened the last time you had a financial problem or a problem with one of your children? Were you surprised by how much fear came out of your mouth? Did you say things that didn't line up with what God's word says about your situation?

It shouldn't have surprised you. That lets you know what's really in your heart. And if you look back, you most likely have been using fear to express yourself. It's grievous that many Christians use words like "afraid" and "scared" to express themselves.

You can get rid of that fear by speaking words of faith—words that express God's goodness and favor in your life. You can drive fear and lack and depression out of your life by speaking the blood of Jesus out of your mouth. But you must say them (faith words) on a consistent basis.

Matthew 15:10-11
When He had called the multitude to Himself, He said to them, "Hear and understand: 11 Not what goes into the mouth defiles a man; but what comes out of the mouth, this defiles a man."

Jesus said this in response to the Pharisees complaining that his disciples did not wash their hands before eating. He used this complaint to explain that true defilement doesn't come from food you put in your mouth. (He wasn't saying that you don't need to wash your hands before eating; that wasn't the point).

Matthew 15:17-18
Do you not yet understand that whatever enters the mouth goes into the stomach and is eliminated? 18 But those things which proceed out of the mouth come from the heart, and they defile a man.

Defilement of your human spirit comes from what you speak out of your mouth. Our bodies were made to eliminate wastes from what we eat but what we speak goes directly into our spirits. Words are spiritual.

John 6:63
The words that I speak to you are spirit, and they are life.

Our tongue brings good or bad things to pass in our lives. Living by faith is trusting God to the point where everything that comes out of our mouths agrees with His word. You can't trust someone if you don't believe what they say. We are to live like Jesus lived, controlling everything around us by words.

Faith Makes You Well

Let's take a look at another example of what Jesus called faith.

Luke 18:36-42
**Then it happened, as He was coming near Jericho, that a certain blind man sat by the road begging. 36 And hearing a multitude passing by, he asked what it meant. 37 So they told him that Jesus of Nazareth was passing by. 38 And he cried out, saying, "Jesus, Son of David, have mercy on me!"
39 Then those who went before warned him that he should be quiet; but he cried out all the more, "Son of David, have mercy on me!"
40 So Jesus stood still and commanded him to be brought to Him. And when he had come near, He asked him, 41 saying, "What do you want Me to do for you?"
He said, "Lord, that I may receive my sight."
42 Then Jesus said to him, "Receive your sight; your faith has made you well."**

Jesus said the man's faith had made him well. What did the man do? He _said_ "Son of David, have mercy on me!" and "Lord, that I may receive my sight". It was what the man said that Jesus called faith. Jesus called what the centurion soldier did "great faith".

Matthew 8:8-10
The centurion answered and said, "Lord, I am not worthy that You should come under my roof. But only speak a word, and my servant will be healed. 9 For I also am a man under authority, having soldiers under me. And I say to this one, 'Go,' and he goes; and to another, 'Come,' and he comes; and to my servant, 'Do this,' and he does it."

10 When Jesus heard it, He marveled, and said to those who followed, "Assuredly, I say to you, I have not found such great faith, not even in Israel!

This centurion soldier believed in the authority of the spoken word to heal his servant. Jesus called this great faith!

God had to have someone with faith in His spoken word to allow the birth of Jesus. Mary heard the words of an angel, received it and was able to conceive the Word of God in her womb.

Luke 1:30-31
Then the angel said to her, "Do not be afraid, Mary, for you have found favor with God. 31 And behold, you will conceive in your womb and bring forth a Son, and shall call His name JESUS.

What Mary says next will determine the course of history. If she talks doubt and unbelief, there's no way God's word can come to pass in her life—and there is no way she can give birth to the Lamb of God. Her response was, "How can this be, since I do not know a man?".

At first glance, it looks like she doesn't believe what the angel said. But that's not what she said. She simply asked *how* this was going to happen. That's a reasonable question. She didn't say, "Oh, I don't believe that nonsense". She was just curious as to how this would take place.

It must have been an acceptable question because the angel answered her.

Luke 1:35
And the angel answered and said to her,"The Holy Spirit will come upon you, and the power of the Highest will overshadow you; therefore, also, that Holy One who is to be born will be called the Son of God.

Then Mary gave the faith response.

Luke 1:38
Then Mary said, Behold the maidservant of the Lord! Let it be to me according to your word." NKJV

Now compare this to what Zacharias said when this same angel Gabriel announced his wife Elizabeth would give birth to John the Baptist.

Luke 1:13, 18
13 But the angel said to him, "Do not be afraid, Zacharias, for your prayer is heard; and your wife Elizabeth will bear you a son, and you shall call his name John.
…. 18 And Zacharias said to the angel,"How shall I know this? For I am an old man, and my wife is well advanced in years.

Zacharias did not ask how this would happen. He said "how shall I know". The Message translation makes it clear how he flat rejected the word of God spoken by the angel.

Luke 1:18
Zachariah said to the angel, "Do you expect me to believe this? I'm an old man and my wife is an old woman." THE MESSAGE

You know what happened next. God shut his mouth until the baby was born. God had to do this in order to keep his negative, doubt filled words from polluting the atmosphere.

Faith in the Blood of Jesus

Now that we've established that the believer must live by faith and that faith is connected to what we say, the next step is to focus on what we are to have faith in. Lets again look at Galatians 2:20.

I have been crucified with Christ; it is no longer I who live, but Christ lives in me; and the life which I now live in the flesh I live by faith in the Son of God, who loved me and gave Himself for me.

Paul says he lives by faith in Jesus who gave Himself for him. Remember, when the bible refers to Jesus giving Himself for us it's talking about His blood. Leviticus 17:11 says that the life of the flesh is in the blood. Therefore, Jesus gave Himself for us by shedding His blood. So when we read Galatians 2:20 in this light we can say that Paul "lived by faith in Jesus' blood that was shed for him". This is the same Paul who wrote "the just shall live by faith" (Hebrews 10:38).

If you are born again and have been made the righteousness of God (2 Corinthians 5:21) you are the just (righteous). You're supposed to live by faith in Jesus blood. And that means you're supposed to speak the blood or "plead" the blood. The life we now live is by faith in the One who gave his life (blood) for us. "Pleading" is not begging. It is a legal term.

When you enter a "plea" in a courtroom, you are stating that you are guilty or innocent based on evidence. In the next few chapters you'll get all the blood evidence you need; evidence that the blood of Jesus has set you free from all the works of the devil.

4

Life Is In The Blood

"There's power in the blood of Jesus!" This is a truth that is sung about in churches across the nation. If you asked Christians if there is power in the blood of Jesus, most would emphatically say yes. But this is a truth that's not a heart revelation to many. It's just something to say. It's something many Christians occasionally acknowledge or don't really think about at all. The bible says it's the truth you *know* that sets you free.

John 8:32
And you shall *know* the truth, and the truth shall make you free."

The word "know' in John 8:32 is the Greek word "epiginosko". It implies a special participation in the knowledge of something. It's knowledge that perfectly unites the subject with the object. It's not just truth that makes us free, but it's an "active knowledge" in the truth that will make us free. It's the truth that *we participate in* and which becomes an active part of our lives that sets us free.

The truth of the life that's in the blood of Jesus needs to be an active revelation to us in order for it to have any power in our lives. You can plead the blood of Jesus all you want, but results only come when it's a reality. You need to meditate on the truth. Study it, think about it and confess it out of your mouth daily. When you do this, the blood of Jesus will take on a new dimension in your life.

A Dividing Line

I heard a very well known bible teacher refer to John 10:10 as "the dividing line of the scriptures". I agree whole-heartedly with this statement.

John 10:10
The thief does not come except to steal, and to kill, and to destroy. I have come that they may have life, and that they may have it more abundantly.

God gets blamed for so many terrible things. People blame God for making them sick, for causing car accidents and killing loved ones. But if you really believe John 10:10 you can't believe God is behind all these tragedies.

This bible teacher called John 10:10 a "dividing line" because if you believe it you won't be confused about whose responsible for any situation in your life. Anything that steals, kills or destroys came from the thief, our adversary, the devil.

Jesus came to give us life and give it to us <u>abundantly</u>. The word translated life is the greek word "zoe". It means "absolute life" which comes only from God. The word translated "abundantly" is the greek word "perissos". It means "over and above, more than is necessary, superadded or excessive". Jesus came so that we might have the life of God in excess.

The Amplified version of John 10:10 is outstanding.

The thief comes only in order to steal and kill and destroy. I came that they may have and enjoy life, and have it in abundance (to the full, till it overflows)
AMP

Jesus came so that we could live and enjoy life to the full and overflowing. That life was in His blood. How do we receive this abundant life? We must be born again. We must receive Jesus as our savior and substitute for sin and then the life and nature of God is born into us.

2 Corinthians 5:17-18
Therefore, if anyone is in Christ, he is a new creation; old things have passed away; behold, all things have become new. 18 Now all things are of God.

When we receive Jesus as our savior and substitute sin offering, we get a blood transfusion. We receive uncorrupted perfect blood that takes the place of the corrupted, sinful blood we inherited from Adam.(1 Peter 1:18-19, Rom 5:14-19)

Now I do not believe our natural blood changes. The blood that runs through our veins gives life to our physical bodies. The blood of Jesus gives life to our spirits. Ephesians 2:5 says that before we received Christ we were "dead in trespasses". This is talking about spiritual death. We are born in this earth with a spirit that is separated from the life of God. But we are "made alive together with Christ" when we are born-again through the Spirit of God (Eph. 2.5). This being "made alive" must be referring to a different kind of life than the one we already have. Everyone who receives salvation is already alive physically. Jesus blood gives the human spirit a new Holy Spirit DNA!!

We've been redeemed by Jesus' blood (Colossians 1:14). The word "redeemed" means "to be brought back to the original state". We are brought back to the original state that Adam had before he sinned. Adam had the life of God flowing in him. He was so full of the light and life of God that he didn't need clothing. The light that was in him radiated throughout his being that there was no need for a covering. That life was contained in Adam's blood.

I want to give you another "dividing line of the scriptures". It's found in the book of Leviticus.

Leviticus 17:11
For the life of the flesh is in the blood, and I have given it to you upon the altar to make atonement for your souls; for it is the blood that makes atonement for the soul.'

The life of the flesh is in the blood. Blood is a mysterious substance. Somehow it holds life itself. When God breathed life into Adam, that life was deposited and contained in Adam's blood. When someone dies, it's because the life that is in the blood has escaped. If someone is injured and enough blood is lost, they literally bleed to death because *the life is in the blood.*

Jesus came to give us life in abundance and that life was contained in His blood. The life of God was in His blood. Jesus was born with holy, uncorrupted blood. His conception was a supernatural conception.

Luke 1:35
And the angel answered and said to her,"The Holy Spirit will come upon you, and the power of the Highest will overshadow you; therefore, also, that Holy One who is to be born will be called the Son of God.

The Holy Spirit was the divine agent that caused the conception of Jesus. His blood type came directly from God. There was no corrupted human blood in the veins of our savior. In the natural, even after conception the placenta protects the fetus from the mother's blood. Mary's corrupted; death-doomed human blood (the blood that is passed down to everyone through Adam) could not contaminate the blood of Jesus.

It had to be that way. If Jesus had not been born with incorruptible blood, He could not be the perfect substitute for our sins. He could not be the perfect Lamb of God to take away the sins of the world. He would have been born with the same sin nature that you and I are born with because he would have received it from the first Adam. That just wouldn't work. God requires a perfect substitute for man's sin.

2 Cor 5:21
For He made Him who knew no sin to be sin for us, that we might become the righteousness of God in Him.

Adam's sin was passed on to every man born after him. There was no escaping it.

Romans 5:18
Therefore, as through one man's offense judgment came to all men, resulting in condemnation, even so through one Man's righteous act the free gift came to all men, resulting in justification of life.

Acts 17:26
And He has made from one blood every nation of men to dwell on all the face of the earth, and has determined their preappointed times and the boundaries of their dwellings,

The "one blood" here in Acts 17:26 is talking about the blood of Adam. The life of God that was in Adam's blood escaped permanently when Adam rebelled in the garden of Eden. The result was corrupted blood that would be passed on to every human being born after Adam. This corrupted blood causes the sinful nature at birth and man's need for a redeemer. A redeemer is someone who brings you back to the original state.

Redeemed also means "ransomed". Think about a son of a wealthy family. He is living a life of luxury and wants for nothing. Suddenly some wicked person snatches him from his parents and holds him captive. He no longer has the wealth and privileges he had while he was living with his family. He is held in bondage until a ransom is paid. Once the ransom has been paid, he's released and brought back to the original life he once had.

That's a pretty good picture of what happened to the human race when Adam turned his back on God and obeyed the devil. We were kidnapped. The bible says we were under the power of darkness (Colossians 1:13, Ephesians 2:2). *Jesus came to give us our lives back!* Jesus blood has redeemed us and brought us back to the original state Adam had before he sinned. The bible calls this the new creation (2 Corinthians 5:17). The blood of Jesus makes us new creatures. We have God's nature in us.

Hebrews 10:16
"This is the covenant that I will make with them after those days, says the LORD: I will put My laws into their hearts, and in their minds I will write them,"

We have God in our hearts. We have the mind of Christ. You may say, "I've received Jesus as my savior, but I still sin and I still have sinful thoughts. I must not have received this new nature." No, you did receive it. But you received it by faith and you must live it by faith. It always comes back to faith. We live as new creatures by faith. You can't live this new life without the knowledge of God and the faith of God.

Galatians 2:20
I have been crucified with Christ; it is no longer I who live, but Christ lives in me; and the life which I now live in the flesh I live by faith in the Son of God, who loved me and gave Himself for me.

When you apply the blood of Jesus by faith to any situation, you speak the life of God into that situation. Life drives out death. Light drives out darkness. The light of God is synonymous with the life of God. Jesus had the light of God in Him.

John 1:4
In Him was life, and the life was the light of men.

Here we see that the life that was in Jesus was also the light of God. The light of God is the manifestation of the life of God. That's why Adam didn't know he was naked before he sinned. The life of God in his blood produced so much light that you couldn't see his nakedness.

Since Jesus came to give us abundant life and that life was contained in His blood, we can speak the life of God by faith into any situation that has death or darkness in it. Speak the blood into your dark, debt ridden finances. Speak the blood into your sick body. Speak the blood over your depressed mind. Every time you speak (or plead) the blood of Jesus by faith, you release all the redeeming power of that blood to bring life into those things.

But you must do it by faith and you can only have faith in something you have knowledge of. Whatever problem you're facing, you need knowledge that the blood of Jesus has already solved that problem. By meditating on John 10:10, you can boldly say to sickness, lack, depression or fear; *"Jesus came and gave me life in abundance, therefore I plead the blood of Jesus and speak life into my finances, my body, and my thoughts!"*

Things always change for the better when you speak the blood of Jesus in faith. That's why Jesus came and that's why the devil wants you to stay ignorant about the life and power that's His blood. But you're changing that by reading this book. You're gaining practical knowledge about the blood. I encourage you to read other books on the blood. Become a "blood specialist".

The most important book on the blood is the bible. Read God's word searching for blood scriptures. Ask God to give you more revelation on the power of Jesus blood. A good prayer to pray is Ephesians 1:15-20.

Eph 1:15-20
Therefore I also, after I heard of your faith in the Lord Jesus and your love for all the saints, 16 do not cease to give thanks for you, making

mention of you in my prayers: 17 that the God of our Lord Jesus Christ, the Father of glory, may give to you the spirit of wisdom and revelation in the knowledge of Him, 18 the eyes of your understanding being enlightened; that you may know what is the hope of His calling, what are the riches of the glory of His inheritance in the saints, 19 and what is the exceeding greatness of His power toward us who believe, according to the working of His mighty power 20 which He worked in Christ when He raised Him from the dead and seated Him at His right hand in the heavenly places,**

In this prayer, the apostle Paul is asking God to give the church at Ephesus revealed knowledge of the power that raised Jesus from the dead. God raised Jesus "through the blood of the everlasting covenant" (Heb. 13:20). This is a prayer asking God to reveal more knowledge of the power of the blood of Jesus! You and I can pray this prayer.

It was the blood that raised Jesus because that blood still had the life of God in it! Ephesians 2:6 says we were raised up *together* with Jesus and I believe it was through the same incorruptible blood of almighty God.

The blood is what defeated the devil and stripped him of his power. He's terrified of it and of all who know how to apply it. But you must have a working revelation of the blood and it's power in order to apply it. The blood of Jesus is not a rabbits foot or "lucky charm". It's not something you carry around with you, plead every now and then and hope it works sometimes. It's not a game. The blood of Jesus works all the time for believers who are fully persuaded of it's redeeming power!

I practice pleading the blood all the time. Anytime someone in my house starts to get sick, I go right for the blood. I know plenty of healing scriptures but I've had more success just pleading the blood of Jesus over my family and commanding that sickness to leave. They may not look any better immediately, but they're fine by the next morning. We don't have any prolonged sickness in our house because the blood is applied. Praise God!

Won't you join the ranks of the believers who have discovered the life that's in the blood? The blood of Jesus is available to you today. It will be there tomorrow. The blood is alive and in heaven right now speaking for you (Hebrews 12:24). If you ask the Holy Spirit, He will reveal what the blood is speaking about you. And you can speak life into every situation—the life and power that's in the blood!

5

Application of The Blood

Hebrews 2:14-15
Inasmuch then as the children have partaken of flesh and blood, He Himself likewise shared in the same, that through death He might destroy him who had the power of death, that is, the devil, 15 and release those who through fear of death were all their lifetime subject to bondage.

Every time you apply the blood of Jesus to a situation, you are putting all that Jesus has done right in the devil's face. Hebrews 2:14 says that Jesus destroyed the power of the devil with His blood.

Notice that it was through His death that Jesus destroyed the power of the devil. Remember, whenever the bible talks about Jesus death it is referring to His blood. Since the life of the flesh is in the blood, any reference to Jesus dying or giving up His life is talking about the shedding of His blood. I always just replace the word death with blood in my thinking and speaking.

The devil hates it when you plead, apply or sprinkle the blood of Jesus. But there's not a thing he can do about it. The blood has defeated him soundly. He couldn't penetrate the blood of the Passover lamb that the children of Israel applied to their homes and he can't penetrate the blood of our Passover lamb when we apply it to our lives.

1 Corinthians 5:7
Therefore purge out the old leaven, that you may be a new lump, since you truly are unleavened. For indeed Christ, *our Passover*, was sacrificed for us.

I believe that's why there has been so little teaching on the blood of Jesus. The devil has deceived the body of Christ about the blood's importance in our lives. If ministers don't teach on the blood of Jesus, it will not hold it's proper position in the believer's life. The blood becomes common and taken for granted. It's never talked about or applied and the devil is allowed to run roughshod over many Christian's lives simply because they have no knowledge of the power of Jesus blood.

Think about it. It was the blood of Jesus that destroyed the devil and all of his power. Jesus is called "our Passover". The blood of the Passover lamb in the old covenant was able to protect the entire nation of Israel when it was applied to the homes of individual families.

Ex 12:13
Now the blood shall be a sign for you on the houses where you are. And when I see the blood, I will pass over you; and the plague shall not be on you to destroy you when I strike the land of Egypt.

Hebrews 11:28
By faith he kept the Passover and the sprinkling of blood, lest he who destroyed the firstborn should touch them.

Have you applied the blood of Jesus to your house today? Are you keeping the Passover (Jesus and His Word) and the sprinkling (speaking) of the blood for protection? Peter wrote that we are not to neglect the sprinkling of the blood.

1 Peter 1:1-2
who have been chosen according to the foreknowledge of God the Father, through the sanctifying work of the Spirit, for obedience to Jesus Christ and sprinkling by his blood:
NIV

Here in 1 Peter, the sanctifying work of the Holy Spirit causes us to be able to obey Jesus and to be sprinkled with His blood. We cannot forget the work of the Holy Spirit when it comes to the blood. 1 John 5:8 says that the Spirit, the water (the word) and the blood all agree as one on earth.

We as believers need to sprinkle the blood of Jesus on everything. Any area in our lives we see demonic influence should be covered by the blood of Jesus. How do you "sprinkle the blood"? We do it by faith ... speaking faith. The Old Testament is our example for instruction (1 Cor 10:11). By faith, we do what they did in the flesh. We don't sprinkle real blood on ourselves but we speak the blood by faith.

Foolishness or Faith?

Is pleading, applying or sprinkling the blood foolishness or faith? I know many born-again, spirit filled Christians that see no reason to speak about the blood of Jesus. Even many Christians who believe in the power of words and confession do not have a revelation of the power that is delivered to the enemy when the blood of Jesus is spoken.

That's why I wrote this book. A few years ago, God impressed me that I was to become a "blood specialist". I never heard anyone say that. I never heard a preacher call himself a "blood specialist" but it was strong in my spirit. *"I want you to become a blood specialist."* All I knew to do was to study everything I could on the blood of Jesus, ask for revealed knowledge and apply the blood in my own life.

I was also stirred up when I started reading the testimonies about believers who pled the blood on a regular basis and saw many miracles and deliverances in their lives. I thought, "why isn't everyone preaching on the blood all the time?"

1 Corinthians 1:18
For the message of the cross is foolishness to those who are perishing, but to us who are being saved it is the power of God.

Let's take a thoughtful look at 1 Corinthians 1:18. The first word I want to draw your attention to is the word "saved". It's the Greek word *"sozo"*. It means to be preserved or brought into safety. When we are born again we say we are saved. But what are we saved from? We're saved from every thing under the curse. We are safe from anything the devil would try to do to us because we are in covenant with God our Heavenly Father. The devil has no authority over us. We have been delivered from his kingdom and translated into God's kingdom (Col. 1:13}.

The second key word in this verse is "perishing". It means to "destroy fully". I believe you can read this verse at least two ways. One way is that the unsaved person has no understanding of the cross (blood) and as a result he is perishing. The saved person believes in the message of the cross (blood) and that's why they're saved. Most believers would draw that from this verse and it's true.

But there is another principle being revealed in this scripture. It speaks to how we appropriate the blood in our everyday lives. Christians who actively believe in the power of the blood and apply the blood daily are consistently being delivered from all evil and are safe. They honor the blood and it's power. They give it first place in their thinking and speaking.

Christians who view pleading or speaking the blood (the message of the cross) as foolishness are in constant danger of destruction in their lives.

They take the blood for granted. They spend little or no time thinking about what the blood has done for them. They never take communion at home and hardly pay attention when they receive communion at church. As a result they spend no effort in using their faith to appropriate the power of the blood in their lives.

What you spend your time studying will dominate your thought life. What you think about, you will talk about and have faith in.

Consider the following scriptures.

2 Corinthians 4:13
13 And since we have the same spirit of faith, according to what is written, "I believed and therefore I spoke," we also believe and therefore speak,

Romans 10:6-9
6 But the righteousness of faith speaks in this way, "Do not say in your heart, 'Who will ascend into heaven?'" (that is, to bring Christ down from above) 7 or, "'Who will descend into the abyss?'" (that is, to bring Christ up from the dead). 8 But what does it say? "The word is near you, in your mouth and in your heart" (that is, the word of faith which we preach): 9 that if you confess with your mouth the Lord Jesus and believe in your heart that God has raised Him from the dead, you will be saved.

Believing is speaking. Since speaking is the main component of faith, you must speak the blood of Jesus if you want to the blood to work for your safety and deliverance from evil.

I was on a vacation with some people I work with one summer. It was a lovely trip to a Caribbean island. One day we took a flight to another island for the day. None of us were aware of the type of plane we would be flying in. We assumed it would be small but we were all surprised when we saw how small it was.

The plane held only eight passengers and was very narrow. In fact I think my car is wider than the plane we all crammed into that day. What was glaring to me was how everyone joked about calamity. People were saying it was a good thing we were flying low because if the plane did go down it wouldn't have far to go before crashing. They joked about being glad they had revised their wills before they left home. I know some of them were Christians.

Let me tell you friend, joking about destruction will not put the blood of Jesus to work for you. You can't talk one way and believe another.

James 3:11-12
Does a spring send forth fresh water and bitter from the same opening? 12 Can a fig tree, my brethren, bear olives, or a grapevine bear figs? Thus no spring yields both salt water and fresh.

I didn't say anything. I didn't try to correct them because I know they didn't have a revelation of the power of the blood or their own words. But I certainly didn't join into their conversation. I already settled my protection before I got on that plane. I applied the blood of Jesus to that plane.

But I hear Christians talk like that all the time. They joke about things that Jesus has already redeemed them (set free by paying the ransom) from through His blood.

Galatians 3:13
13 Christ has redeemed us from the curse of the law, having become a curse for us (for it is written, "Cursed is everyone who hangs on a tree")

Look at the 28th chapter of Deuteronomy. Many Christians study and confess the first part … the blessings. But I want you to look at the curses. Get a few translations and study them. You will be struck at how many tragedies that people experience are listed under the curse.

I remember when the little girl from Utah was kidnapped right from her own home a few years ago. It was in all the national news. Well, because of this story, the media decided that we should know about every child abducted in this county. You would have thought that kids were being snatched left and right. I found out later that child abductions were actually *down*! It's just that more of them were making the national headlines.

I have three daughters. Two were adults but one was only 12. I started letting fear get in me about her being abducted. Thoughts would come that I failed to resist and before I knew it I was almost afraid to let her out of my sight.

Then one day I was reading the 28th chapter of Deuteronomy. I make it a point to read what I'm redeemed from. And there it was, child abduction.

Deuteronomy 28:41
You shall beget sons and daughters, but they shall not be yours; *for they shall go into captivity.*

Child abduction is under the curse and according to Galatians 3:13, Christ has redeemed us from the curse. I immediately declared *"I'm redeemed from child abduction. I plead the blood!"*. Now when I sprinkle the blood on my daughters, it means something. I have a promise to attach my faith in the blood to. I found some other specific situations that were included under the curse in Deuteronomy 28. They are:

Identity Theft vs.33
Robbery vs.28-29
Confusion vs.28

Fear vs.66
Lack vs.38-40
Terrorism vs.49-52

Applying the Blood

Why must we apply the blood of Jesus? You may say, "Sure I believe in the blood but it was applied to me when I got saved. I don't need to keep talking about it". In 1 Corinthians 5:7 Paul calls Christ "our Passover lamb". Since the Old Testament is our example, we should look at what Israel did with the first Passover lamb.

We see that they ate the flesh and applied the blood to the top and sides of the doors of their homes. But how can we eat the flesh of Jesus Christ, our Passover lamb? Jesus called Himself "the bread of life" in John 6:35. Jesus is also called word made flesh in John 1:1.14. Jesus is the Word of God and He is the bread of life. We eat His flesh by consuming the word of God.

How do we apply the blood of our Passover lamb? We speak it over our lives. Remember, it did the children of Israel no good if they just killed the Passover lamb and ate it. They had to apply the blood on the door of their homes, where they kept their families and possessions.

Now, we can understand what Peter meant when he said we were chosen "to Christ and be sprinkled with His blood" (1Peter 1:2NASB). We are called to obey God's word and to sprinkle the blood of Jesus. Hebrews 12:24 says the "blood of sprinkling *speaks* better things than that of Abel". We are to sprinkle the blood by speaking it over things. Every day we can say, *"In Jesus name I sprinkle the blood of Jesus over myself, my family, my possessions, my job, my relationships, my neighborhood, my finances and my body".*

Keeping the Blood First Place

Are you applying the blood to your life on a daily basis? Are you keeping the blood of Jesus of first importance?

1 Corinthians 15:3-4
For I delivered to you first of all that which I also received: that Christ died for our sins according to the Scriptures, and that He was buried, and that He rose again the third day according to the Scriptures,

The apostle Paul put the death, burial and resurrection of Jesus first. It was the first revelation he received and the first he delivered to the Corinthian church, a carnal church that had lots of carnal problems. I believe we would have more constant victory in our lives if we put the blood first in our thinking and speaking.

I learned a long time ago to ask myself what the word of God says about any situation I face in my life. But now I ask myself what the blood of Jesus says about my situation. You see, the blood of Jesus is in heaven speaking. The blood is alive and speaking about you and me.

Hebrews 12:22-24
But you have come to Mount Zion and to the city of the living God, the heavenly Jerusalem, to an innumerable company of angels, 23 to the general assembly and church of the firstborn who are registered in heaven, to God the Judge of all, to the spirits of just men made perfect, 24 to Jesus the Mediator of the new covenant, and to the blood of sprinkling that speaks better things than that of Abel.

The bible says the blood of Jesus is speaking blood. It's alive right now before the throne of God and it's speaking. It's speaking about you and me. What is it speaking? It's saying, "they're redeemed from the curse (Gal.3:13) … they're the righteousness of God (Rom.5:9) … they've received the abundance of God's favor and they reign as kings in this life

(Rom.5:17AMP) ..." Well if the blood of Jesus is saying this for you and me, we should be agreeing with the blood.

1 John 5:8
And there are three that bear witness on earth: the Spirit, the water, and the blood; and these three agree as one.

This scripture says the Holy Spirit and the Word of God agree with the blood of Jesus. The words translated "bear witness" means to testify. You testify with words. Water in the bible often refers to the Word of God.

Ephesians 5:25-26
Husbands, love your wives, just as Christ also loved the church and gave Himself for her, 26 that He might sanctify and cleanse her with the washing of water by the word,

I believe the water in 1 John 5:8 refers to the Word of God.

How To Agree with The Blood

This act of agreeing with the blood is very important in the walk of faith. We're told that we are to live by faith, not just "do faith" once in a while. To demonstrate how to agree with the blood, let me give you an example of not agreeing with the blood.

Galatians 3:13 says we're redeemed from the curse through Jesus shed blood ... **"for it is written, cursed is everyone who hangs on a tree"**. I believe that Jesus' blood is in heaven is speaking that I've been redeemed from the curse. When I study what's under the curse in Deuteronomy 28, I find *madness* or *craziness* in verse 28.

Once I find that craziness is under the curse I no longer can make statements like "they're driving me crazy". The blood says I'm redeemed from craziness. The Word says I'm redeemed from craziness. The Holy Spirit is in agreement with the blood and the word, so He says I'm redeemed from craziness.

I'm the only one that can be out of agreement and I have the deciding voice of what will prevail in my life. All the forces of God are behind me to deliver me. But I must agree with the blood. Let's take the favor of God as another example.

Ps 5:12-6:1
For You, O LORD, will bless the righteous;
With favor You will surround him as with a shield.

We see here that a shield of God's favor surrounds righteous people. That's a powerful revelation. Think about it; if you're righteous you have a shield of God's supernatural favor wrapped around you everywhere you go. It doesn't matter how people treat you, the word of God says that favor surrounds those who are righteous and that's what you should say about yourself.

The word of God and the blood of Jesus says you're righteous.

Rom 5:9
Much more then, having now been justified (made righteous) by His blood, we shall be saved from wrath through Him.

If you are made righteous through the blood and God surrounds the righteous with favor, you have scriptural basis to declare "By the blood of Jesus, God's favor surrounds me as a shield". Saying anything otherwise is <u>not</u> agreeing with the blood. If you have a revelation of God's favor through the blood of Jesus you will never be concerned about people liking you. You won't be offended if someone doesn't speak to you. If you have faith that you have God's favor surrounding you, what difference does it make if someone speaks to you or not. You speak to them because you're confident that you have God's favor.

The Power of Confession

Matt 12:35-37
A good man out of the good treasure of his heart brings forth good things, and an evil man out of the evil treasure brings forth evil things. 36 But I say to you that for every idle word men may speak, they will give account of it in the day of judgment. 37 For by your words you will be justified, and by your words you will be condemned."

You have the power to bring good things to pass in your life. God made you that way. The bible says that you were created in the image of God. God creates through words and man creates through words. It's true because the word of God says so. The important thing to understand is that this is a spiritual law and it works whether you believe it or not. Your words are either working for you or against you but they are working in your life.

So why not get them to work for you? Why not use your God-given creative power to bring "good" things to pass in your life? After all, you were created for this. The word "good" in Matthew 12:35 means "something that is beneficial in its effect". The word "evil" means "of a bad nature of condition".

What are "Good Things"?

If we are to bring "good things" to pass by speaking them out of our mouths, then we must know what those "good things" are. We cannot just assume we know what's good by our own reasoning. This is where many Christians stumble. They base their lives on their own view of righteousness and not the righteousness of God. Jesus made it clear how we can know what to say.

Matt 16:17-19

Jesus answered and said to him, "Blessed are you, Simon Bar-Jonah, for flesh and blood has not revealed this to you, but My Father who is in heaven. 18 And I also say to you that you are Peter, and on this rock I will build My church, and the gates of Hades shall not prevail against it. 19 And I will give you the keys of the kingdom of heaven, and whatever you bind on earth will be bound in heaven, and whatever you loose on earth will be loosed in heaven."

I've always heard Matthew 16:17, 18 and Matthew 16:19 preached as a separate message. Jesus is telling Peter in the 17th and 18th verses that it is God in heaven that revealed His identity as the Christ, the son of the living God. And it was through this revelation knowledge that His church would be built. This is a powerful truth and the foundational scripture for a believer to seek after revelation knowledge.

Matthew 16:19 is our "binding and loosing" scripture. To get a clearer understanding of this scripture let's look at the Amplified version.

Matt 16:19
**19 I will give you the keys of the kingdom of heaven; and whatever you bind (declare to be improper and unlawful) on earth must be what is already bound in heaven; and whatever you loose (declare lawful) on earth must be what is already loosed in heaven.
AMP**

For years I read the King James version of Matthew 16:19 and thought that we had the power to bind (forbid) and loose (allow) things in heaven. That didn't make any sense to me. That would mean that every believer could change what's going on in heaven by what they said here on earth. Talk about confusion! But when I read the Amplified version, I understood exactly what Jesus was saying. He was giving us the key to unlock the kingdom of heaven that's on the inside of every born again believer.

In this scripture Jesus is telling believers how to talk. He says we should declare what is already allowed in heaven. We should bind by forbidding what's not allowed in heaven. But how do we know what's allowed in heaven? He told us in verse seventeen. It's by revelation knowledge.

The kingdom of God is within you if you're born again.

Luke 17:21
nor will they say,'See here!' or 'See there!' For indeed, the kingdom of God is within you."

Days of Heaven upon the earth

You're in two places at once. Your body is here on earth. Your spirit is also here on earth contained in your body. But your spirit is also joined with Jesus seated at the right hand of God.

Eph 2:4-7
even when we were dead in trespasses, made us alive together with Christ (by grace you have been saved), 6 and raised us up together, and made us sit together in the heavenly places in Christ Jesus,

Your spirit is in contact with heaven while you're body is here on the earth. Jesus gave us the keys to unlock heaven on the inside of us. Through the revelation knowledge of God's word, we can know what's allowed or disallowed in heaven. Then we know what to allow in our lives by the words we speak.

That's what Jesus is saying in Matthew 16:17-19. For example, if we know that poverty is not allowed in heaven, we shouldn't allow it in our lives by declaring that we're poor no matter what our circumstances look like. We should declare what is in heaven. There's abundance in heaven, so we say "I have abundance and no lack".

It grieves me that many Christians still refuse to say what heaven says about them. You can have days of heaven on earth.

Deut 11:18, 21
"Therefore you shall lay up these words of mine in your heart and in your soul, and bind them as a sign on your hand, and they shall be as frontlets between your eyes.
21 that your days and the days of your children may be multiplied in the land of which the LORD swore to your fathers to give them, like the days of the heavens above the earth.

When you speak on earth what is already allowed in heaven, you bring heaven on earth in your life and environment. When you forbid on earth what is forbidden in heaven you bind the devil from having control in your life. The bible says that the blood of Jesus is in heaven speaking better things than that of Abel.

1 John 5:6-8
For there are three that bear witness in heaven: the Father, the Word, and the Holy Spirit; and these three are one. 8 And there are three that bear witness on earth: the Spirit, the water, and the blood; and these three agree as one.

I believe the blood of Jesus bears witness on earth as believers speak what the blood speaks in heaven. The blood speaks all that redemption has provided. It speaks that we have been redeemed from the curse of the law. It speaks that we are healed, prosperous, victorious, full of joy and free of fear. It speaks that we have favor with God and man. It speaks that God blesses all that we set our hands to.

How do I know the blood is speaking these things in heaven? It comes through revelation knowledge of God's word. The more revelation you have on the subject of the blood, the more power the blood will produce in your life.

The bible says that Jesus had favor with God and with men.

Luke 2:52
And Jesus increased in wisdom and stature, and in favor with God and men.

Notice it says that Jesus increased in favor as He increased in wisdom. The word of God is the wisdom of God.

Luke 11:49
49 Therefore the wisdom of God also said,'I will send them prophets and apostles, and some of them they will kill and persecute,'

Deut 4:5-6
"Surely I have taught you statutes and judgments, just as the LORD my God commanded me, that you should act according to them in the land which you go to possess. 6 Therefore be careful to observe them; for this is your wisdom and your understanding in the sight of the peoples who will hear all these statutes.

The more we increase in revelation of God's word, the more we'll walk in God's divine nature and escape the corruption in this world (2 Peter1:2-4). It's not a matter of God giving us more of His divine nature when we study His word. It's that we know what to expect from our covenant. It's one thing to know you have a covenant with God. It's another to know what that covenant says you're entitled to.

The more revelation we have on the blood of Jesus, the more power we'll walk in when we apply the blood. Many Christians have misunderstood "pleading" the blood. They think that by "pleading" the blood of Jesus they are begging God to do something he hasn't made up His mind to do. This is far from the truth.

The word "plead" is the same word we use when we say someone entered a "plea" in a court of law. It is their petition or argument. It is their formal statement of their justification. And that's exactly what you do when you plead the blood of Jesus. You are declaring before the three worlds; heaven, earth and hell (Philippians 2:10) all the blood has done. And it has done a lot.

When we plead the blood of Jesus in faith, power is released and devils tremble.

James 1:5-6
But let him ask in faith, with no doubting, for he who doubts is like a wave of the sea driven and tossed by the wind.
NKJV

There is so much the blood has done for us my friend. If you study the bible looking for blood revelations, I believe it would be a search you could not exhaust. Remember, God is pleased when we seek after Him, believing that we will be rewarded (Hebrews 11:6). I believe there are three major areas that Christians should seek knowledge about the blood. These three areas seem to be the root of many problems faced by believers today. They are *fear*, *sickness* and *lack*.

6

"No Fear" Through The Blood

Heb 2:14-16
14 Inasmuch then as the children have partaken of flesh and blood, He Himself likewise shared in the same, that through death He might destroy him who had the power of death, that is, the devil, 15 and release those who through fear of death were all their lifetime subject to bondage.

The blood of Jesus has defeated fear. The words "through death" in Hebrews 2:14 refer to the shedding of Jesus blood. The 15th verse states that His blood was shed to release mankind from the bondage of the "fear of death". This is the fear that came as a result of spiritual death, not the fear of dying.

Fear is an enemy. It is not something to be tolerated or put up with. Every believer should resist fear simply because Jesus shed his blood to destroy fear. It's a dishonor to the blood of our Lord Jesus Christ to put up with fear. Many Christians don't understand this. They not only put up with fear, but they invite fear into their lives all the time by talking about it.

Expressions like, "I'm afraid not" or "that almost scared me to death" are not just meaningless words. They are fear based.

In order to understand why fear is an enemy we must understand where and how it came into the human race to begin with. In order to do this we must go back to the book of beginnings. When man was created he had no fear.

Gen 1:26-27
26 Then God said,"Let Us make man in Our image, according to Our likeness; let them have dominion over the fish of the sea, over the birds of the air, and over the cattle, over all the earth and over every creeping thing that creeps on the earth."
NKJV

Man was made in God's own image. He was created to have dominion in the earth. No fear is mentioned. Man had the eternal life of God breathed into him and that life was contained in his blood.

Lev 17:11
11 For the life of the flesh is in the blood,

Adam was full of the life of God and the love of God. There is no fear in love (1 John 4:18). Adam had no fear until he disobeyed God and allowed spiritual death to enter his blood.

Gen 2:16-17
"Of every tree of the garden you may freely eat; 17 but of the tree of the knowledge of good and evil you shall not eat, for in the day that you eat of it you shall surely die."

The words "you shall surely die" refers to spiritual death, not physical death. We know that Adam did not die physically right after he disobeyed God. He lived to be a ripe old age physically, but spiritual death took hold immediately. And something else happened right away. Adam immediately moved away from God because of fear.

Gen 3:10
So he said, "I heard Your voice in the garden, and I was afraid because I was naked; and I hid myself."

The revelation of Adam and Eve and the fall of man is a key foundation to understanding the power of the blood of Jesus. After they sinned, something happened to their relationship with almighty God. They walked in fear instead of faith. They moved away from God instead of towards Him. That's what fear does. It makes you move away from God. It makes you doubt that God is for you and wants the best for you. When you have no confidence in God's favor you miss out on many of God's blessings.

Heb 11:6
But without faith it is impossible to please Him, for he who comes to God must believe that He is, and that He is a rewarder of those who diligently seek Him.

Adam and Eve's blood became corrupted as a result of the fall. The life of God contained in their blood left and fear was the result. That's the problem with man today; corrupted blood. Death passed from the first Adam to every human being that has been born since.

Romans 5:12
Therefore, just as through one man sin entered the world, and death through sin, and thus death spread to all men, because all sinned.

The good news is that the last Adam, Jesus, "destroyed him who had the power of death" and released us from the spirit of fear.

The Curse of Fear

Galatians 3:13 says Christ has redeemed us from the curse by His blood. Did you know that fear is listed under the curse?

Deut 28:66
Your life shall hang in doubt before you; you shall fear day and night, and have no assurance of life.

Earlier, I mentioned that we don't have to put up with anything that is listed under the curse. We're already redeemed from the curse. One meaning of the word redeemed is "to be brought back to the original state". This is very striking to our thinking. All we have to do is look at how Adam was before he sinned. That's what the blood of Jesus has purchased for us. We have been brought back to Adam before the garden.

1 John 4:18
There is no fear in love; but perfect love casts out fear, because fear involves torment. But he who fears has not been made perfect in love.

God is love. There is no fear in God. By the blood of Jesus, we have been redeemed from fear and we have power to defeat fear in our lives. How do we do this? By speaking the blood against fear. When you are gripped by fear, plead the blood. When your family is fearful, plead the blood.

Fear is a manifestation of the devil's work. It's the result of believing the devil can do something to you he has no right to do because of the blood of Jesus. When you plead the blood of Jesus against fear the devil has no choice but to leave. He hates the blood. Simply say *"Fear, you leave me now. I put the blood of Jesus against you. I'm redeemed from fear according to Deuteronomy 28:66 and Galatians 3:13."*

God did not create us to fear. We are not built for it. Our bodies were not made to fear. Look at how our bodies respond to stress. Stress is the result of worry. Worry is just another word for fear. Worry is meditating on negative things; most of which have not happened yet.

When you're in faith and meditating on the precious promises of God's word, there is no worry. The bible tells us what will happen to our bodies if we trust God and free ourselves from fear and worry.

Prov 3:5-8
Trust in the LORD with all your heart,

And lean not on your own understanding;
6 In all your ways acknowledge Him,
And He shall direct your paths.
7 Do not be wise in your own eyes;
Fear the LORD and depart from evil.
8 *It will be health to your flesh,*
And strength to your bones.

Notice that the result of trusting in the Lord is health to all our flesh. Man was created to trust God. God made our bodies and He knows how to keep our bodies working properly. We are not made to worry about our lives. We have a Father God in heaven to take care of us. All throughout the word of God we are told to trust in the Lord not in ourselves.

When fear rears it's ugly head in your life, don't accept it. Don't put up with it. Your redemption in the blood of Jesus has delivered you from it. Boldly say "I'm redeemed from you spirit of fear by the blood of Jesus". Remember the devil hates the blood. He doesn't want you to mention it. But you must get into the habit of honoring and speaking the blood all day every day. The results will astound you.

Anytime I've noticed problems becoming the bigger in my life, I can trace it back to not honoring and pleading the blood on a consistent basis. And the reason I'm not honoring the blood is because I've been trying to solve my own problems. That's pride. When you try to solve your own problems by figuring them out yourself, you're in pride.

James 4:6 says "God resists the proud". God has no choice but to resist you. If you're sitting at the controls of your life, He won't move you aside and take over. You have to make that decision yourself. We are instructed to humble ourselves in 1 Peter 5:6. God will not make us humble.

Eph 2:6
and raised us up together, and made us sit together in the heavenly places in Christ Jesus.

See yourself spiritually seated in heaven in Christ Jesus. See yourself above fear. See the blood of sprinkling before the throne of God speaking for you (Heb 12:24). And know that you are there and have a right to be there because of His precious blood. Fear is no match for you when you speak the blood against it. The more you speak the blood, the more those fearful thoughts will shrink. The reason most Christians don't plead the blood consistently is because of pride. I'm convinced that you won't plead the blood of Jesus when you're in pride. As I mentioned, pride is simply trusting in yourself and not in God who raises the dead.

Something else happens when you resist fear. Remember Hebrews 2:14 says that through death (His blood) Jesus destroyed the devil's power. The devil is defeated through the blood of Jesus. When you resist fear you enforce the devil's defeat.

Phil 1:27-28
and not in any way terrified by your adversaries, which is to them a proof of perdition, but to you of salvation, and that from God.

The word "perdition" means "destruction". We know the devil is our adversary (1 Peter 5:8). This is saying that we are not to be terrified or fearful of anything the devil throws our way. This is "proof" or evidence of the destruction he's already suffered through the blood of Jesus. Every time we refuse to fear, it's more proof the devil is defeated and has no power in our lives.

Plead the blood of Jesus against fear. Do it everyday. Don't let up because our adversary never lets up.

1 Peter 5:8-9
8 Be of sober spirit, be on the alert. Your adversary, the devil, prowls about like a roaring lion, seeking someone to devour. 9 But *resist him, firm in your faith,*
NASB

7

Healed By The Blood

Our household has had no sickness or disease for years. This is truly a blessing from God.

My wife was a very sickly child. She got ear infections all the time. As an adult, she would routinely suffer from various ailments throughout the year. I had an allergy known as hay fever for as long as I could remember. During the spring and fall I would have sneezing attacks that would make it difficult for me to work sometimes. I didn't like taking medication because it would make me tired. I would have to take it on the really bad days though.

I live in the Northeast and there are days in the spring when you can see the pollen clearly on your car. If you've ever suffered from the hay fever allergy, you know this means you're in for a rough day. It feels as though you have a little man with a feather in your nose that won't stop tickling you.

But I haven't suffered from hay fever in years or any other sickness or allergy. My wife no longer has seasonal illnesses. We have three children. Two are grown, but the youngest is still in high school. I can't remember the last time she had to stay home because of an illness.

I don't believe there is any other reason for this other than appropriating the blood of Jesus in our home. Every day I apply, place and sprinkle the blood of Jesus on my home for protection against any sickness or disease in my household.

Jesus bore the curse for us. That includes every sickness and every disease both known and unknown. At the time of this writing there's a lot of concern in the world about a virus called "the bird flu". This flu has the potential to kill millions of people. One report I read said that it could wipe out one sixth of the world's population.

If I did not have a covenant with God, this would concern me. But it doesn't concern me. It shouldn't concern you either if you're a born again child of God, redeemed by the blood of the Lamb. Jesus already bore the bird flu and any other flu that comes along forever. You must focus your mind on that truth and not let any news reports of devastating viruses influence you. Isaiah 26:3 says God will keep us in perfect peace (wholeness) if our minds stay on Him. We need to keep our minds fixed on the blood of Jesus and what that blood has done for our health.

Galatians 3:13
13 Christ has redeemed us from the curse of the law, having become a curse for us (for it is written, "Cursed is everyone who hangs on a tree"),

Sickness and disease are listed under the curse in the 28th chapter of Deuteronomy. Some terrible things are mentioned in this chapter. But if you're not sure about any specific disease being covered in the curse, just look at the 61st verse.

Deuteronomy 28:61
61 Also every sickness and every plague, which is not written in this Book of the Law, will the LORD bring upon you until you are destroyed.

That means every sickness and disease that will ever come on this earth is included in the curse.

It's important to understand why the translation in Deuteronomy 28:61 indicates that God is the one causing the sickness and disease. Actually a correct translation would say that God would allow every sickness and every plaque to come upon you. Since there is no permissive tense in the Hebrew language, all the curses are written as though God puts them on people. But that's not true. He only allows them and that only happens when we disobey His laws.

Every curse listed in the 28th chapter of Deuteronomy is a result of not obeying the voice of the Lord our God. It doesn't mean God puts the curse on you, only that He will allow curses (which are already here) to come on you. In other words the protection of the Lord from these curses is removed.

That's like a parent who tells their child not to touch a hot stove. They tell the child that they'll not be harmed if they stay away from the stove but if they touch it, they'll get burned. Well, the child decides to touch the stove anyway. The parent comes running when the child cries out as the pain surges through their fingers. They got burned and now their little body is damaged.

Well, you wouldn't say that the parent burned the child. They told the child that they would get hurt if they disobeyed their command and they were right. But they didn't cause the burn. It was disobedience to the voice of Mom and Dad that got little Timmy in trouble, but you can't blame his parents for causing that burn.

That's the way many Christians think about sickness and disease. They think that God is trying to teach them something and that's why they're sick. They must have done something wrong and God is punishing them with this terrible disease to make them humble.

While it's true that sickness and disease are a result of sin, its also true that Jesus blood redeemed us from both. And when you confess your sins He's faithful and just to forgive you and cleanse you from all unrighteousness (1John 1:9). Just confess your sins when you disobey and allow the blood to wash you clean.

You don't have to stay sick one second longer than it takes you to confess your sins if you miss it. But if you don't believe it's God's will for you to be well, you'll never call on Him to be your healer. You won't expect someone who made you sick to heal you if you think they want you sick in the first place.

Redeemed From Sickness

Sickness is a curse. It's not a blessing from God. The only person who could possibly think that sickness is a blessing is someone who's never been sick. God doesn't teach us through sickness. It's not His nature. God is a giver not a taker. His nature is giving. He is love.

Sickness is a thief and that's the devil's nature. It steals time we would spend enjoying life. It steals finances. It steals productivity. It steals from your family's quality of life. Sickness does not add to anyone's life. It's only job is to kill, steal and destroy.

John 10:10
The thief does not come except to steal, and to kill, and to destroy. I have come that they may have life, and that they may have it more abundantly.

One scripture makes it very clear where sickness comes from and who's responsible for it. It's found in the book of Acts.

Acts 10:38
… how God anointed Jesus of Nazareth with the Holy Spirit and with power, who went about doing good and healing all who were oppressed by the devil, for God was with Him.

Notice that God anointed Jesus to *heal* all who were oppressed by the devil. The devil is the one who makes people sick, not God. God and the devil are not working together. God is not double-minded. He would not send and anoint Jesus to destroy the works of the devil and then enlist the devil to make people sick. Jesus came to give us life in abundance. He shed His precious, holy, uncorrupted blood to set us free from everything under the curse.

Another verse that identifies the author of sickness and disease is Luke 13.

Luke 13:11, 16
11 And behold, there was a woman who had a spirit of infirmity eighteen years, and was bent over and could in no way raise herself up ... 16 So ought not this woman, being a daughter of Abraham, whom Satan has bound—think of it—for eighteen years, be loosed from this bond on the Sabbath?"

Apply The Blood for Your Healing

Healing is not mystery. It's part of our redemption. When Jesus hung on the cross and became our sin substitute, His blood healed us of every sickness and disease under the curse.

1 Peter 2:24
who Himself bore our sins in His own body on the tree, that we, having died to sins, might live for righteousness—by whose stripes you were healed.

Notice that Jesus stripes (blood) healed us at the same time He bore our sins. Sickness and disease entered the earth when sin entered the earth. Adam sinned, his blood became corrupted and he fell short of the glory of God. Jesus bore every sickness and disease for mankind on the cross. The 53rd chapter of Isaiah brings this to light in the Amplified version.

Isa 53:4-5
Surely He has borne our griefs (sicknesses, weaknesses, and distresses) and carried our sorrows and pains [of punishment], yet we [ignorantly] considered Him stricken, smitten, and afflicted by God [as if with leprosy].
5 But He was wounded for our transgressions, He was bruised for our guilt and iniquities; the chastisement [needful to obtain] peace and well-being for us was upon Him, and with the stripes [that wounded] Him we are healed and made whole.
AMP

Healing has already been provided for us through the blood of Jesus. You may say, "then why do I still get sick?". Because you still accept sickness. Just like your salvation was already settled before you received Jesus as your personal savior, your healing is already settled. You must receive Jesus as your healer the same way you received Him as your savior.

You must confess with your mouth that *"by the stripes (blood) of Jesus, I am healed"*. Everything God has provided for us must be appropriated in our lives on purpose. It will not just fall on you because you're a Christian. You must accept it, receive it and confess it out of your mouth. We have an enemy and he wants to kill, steal and destroy everything in our lives.

When you speak the blood for your healing, you release all of God's power that has already healed you. You say, *"by the blood of Jesus I am healed. Satan, take your hands off my body. Jesus blood defeated you 2000 years ago, therefore I defeated you 2000 years ago. I enforce your defeat and put the blood against you now!"*

There is nothing the devil can do to you when you use the blood. If he could have stopped the power of the blood, it would not have raised Jesus from the dead (Hebrews 13:20). It would not have kept the destroyer from the homes of the children of Israel.

Exodus 12:13
Now the blood shall be a sign for you on the houses where you are. And when I see the blood, I will pass over you; and the plague shall not be on you to destroy you when I strike the land of Egypt.

Just like the children of Israel applied the blood of the Passover lamb to their doorposts, you must apply the blood of Jesus to your life with your tongue. Do it today. Do it right now. Say, *"In the name of Jesus, I apply the blood of Jesus to my home, my family, my possessions* **and my body***"*. Keep the blood on your lips. Put it on everything by faith. Don't try it. Do it by faith, expecting the blood's power to work for you and your family.

The more you speak about the blood and gain revelation knowledge of the blood, the more faith you will have in the blood. And the gates of hell cannot prevail against you.

Matthew 16:16-18
Simon Peter answered and said,"You are the Christ, the Son of the living God."
17 Jesus answered and said to him, "Blessed are you, Simon Bar-Jonah, for flesh and blood has not revealed this to you, but My Father who is in heaven. 18 And I also say to you that you are Peter, and on this rock (revealed knowledge) I will build My church, and the gates of Hades shall not prevail against it.

8

Abundance Through The Blood

2 Corinthians 8:9
9 For you know the grace of our Lord Jesus Christ, that though He was rich, yet for your sakes He became poor, that you through His poverty might become rich.

No subject in all of Christianity gets more criticism than the belief that God wants you to have material wealth. Even the word "prosperity" has been watered down to mean that God will only meet your needs. Many believers think that if they have a good job, can pay their mortgage note on time, they have two cars in the garage (with notes on each), they're prospering the way God wants them to.

We cannot measure what God wants for us based on what the world says or what religious tradition says. The reason many believers don't have the mind of Christ where money is concerned is because they have no interest in it. If you're not interested in God's will for your life, you'll never find it. It won't just "come to you" someday.

That's the way the system works. God is the rewarder of those who diligently seek Him (Heb.11:6). You are designed to increase in the things you focus on. You will increase in whatever thoughts dominate your mind. It's a spiritual law. Some call it "the law of increase" and it's found in the fourth chapter of Mark's gospel. Here is the Amplified translation.

Mark 4:24-25
24 And He said to them, Be careful what you are hearing. The measure[of thought and study] you give [to the truth you hear] will be the measure[of virtue and knowledge] that comes back to you—and more [besides] will be given to you who hear. 25 For to him who has will more be given; and from him who has nothing, even what he has will be taken away [by force],
AMP

The more you give yourself to study of the word of God on material wealth, the more truth and revelation you receive. And when you get a revelation of what belongs to you in the kingdom of God, nothing can stop you from getting it. Jesus said that revelation knowledge (knowledge that is revealed in your spirit from heaven) is the key to unlock the kingdom of God (Matthew16:16-19). The kingdom of God is God's way of doing things. It is manifested in your life when you let God's word reign in everything you say and do.

Matthew 16:16-19
16 Simon Peter answered and said,"You are the Christ, the Son of the living God."
17 Jesus answered and said to him, "Blessed are you, Simon Bar-Jonah, for flesh and blood has not revealed this to you, but My Father who is in heaven. 18 And I also say to you that you are Peter, and on this rock I will build My church, and the gates of Hades shall not prevail against it. 19 And I will give you the keys of the kingdom of heaven, and whatever you bind on earth will be bound in heaven, and whatever you loose on earth will be loosed in heaven."

I know I've mentioned these verses earlier in this book, but it's worth looking at them again. These four verses reveal a powerful truth about operating in the kingdom of God. This is worth dedicating a whole book to, but I'll just give you my short explanation of what our Lord is saying here.

Jesus is saying that revelation knowledge is knowledge that comes from heaven. It is not received through the human senses. God reveals this knowledge to our spirits. See 1Corinthians 2:9-12. The church is to be built on revelation knowledge, not sense knowledge. God reveals what is in heaven through the Holy Spirit by revelation knowledge in His word. When we receive a revelation on something from heaven, we'll know what is forbidden (bound) or allowed (loosed) in heaven, and that's what we should bind and loose in our lives.

For example, if we allow the Holy Spirit to reveal through the word of God how heaven's economy works, we'll know what to forbid and allow in our financial lives. God wants us to operate in the kingdom of heaven economic system. Jesus said the kingdom of God is inside us (Luke 17:21). We unlock that kingdom through revelation knowledge. Through revelation knowledge, we know what to allow and forbid in our lives. And the gates of hell shall not prevail against us.

We are really in two places at once. Ephesians 2:6 says that we have been raised up together with Christ in heavenly places. Colossians 1:13 says that we have been "translated" into the kingdom of God's dear son. Our spirits are in Christ Jesus in heaven and they are in our bodies here on earth. What we say determines whether we release the kingdom of heaven in our lives.

God has made us free moral agents and if you're not interested in His word, there will be a veil over it and you won't be able to understand it.

2 Corinthians 3:14-15
But their minds were blinded. For until this day the same veil remains unlifted in the reading of the Old Testament, because the veil is taken away in Christ. 15 But even to this day, when Moses is read, a veil lies on their heart.

So let's approach God's word with unveiled hearts and allow the Holy Spirit to reveal the truth about what he wants for us financially. I don't want wealth just because I want to be a big shot or because I want to be stronger than others if the economy goes bad. I want to be in God's perfect will. I realize I can't be a strong witness to others or help anyone without God's power to get wealth operating in my life.

Redeemed From Poverty and Lack

Galatians 3:13-14 is a foundational scripture every born-again Christian should meditate on daily.

Galatians 3:13-14
13 Christ has redeemed us from the curse of the law, having become a curse for us (for it is written, "Cursed is everyone who hangs on a tree"), 14 that the blessing of Abraham might come upon the Gentiles in Christ Jesus, that we might receive the promise of the Spirit through faith.

Poverty is a curse. It's not a blessing from God. It's included in the curse outlined in the 28th chapter of Deuteronomy.

Deut 28:38-40
38 "You will plant much but harvest little, for locusts will eat your crops. 39 You will plant vineyards and care for them, but you will not drink the wine or eat the grapes, for worms will destroy the vines. NLT

We've been redeemed from poverty and lack by the blood of Jesus. Again, the word "redeemed" means "brought back to the original state". The original state of man when he was created was not poor. Adam wanted for nothing. God provided everything he needed or wanted.

The blood of Jesus has redeemed us from the curse of poverty and has brought us into the blessing of Abraham. The bible calls Abraham the father of those who walk by faith (Romans 4:12). If we are Christ's, we are Abraham's seed according to Galatians 3:29. We are Christ's and we've been raised up together with Him through the blood of the everlasting covenant (Hebrews 13:20).

Since those who are of faith are blessed *with* believing Abraham (Gal. 3:9), we need to look at how Abraham was blessed.

The bible says that Abraham was extremely rich (Genesis 13:2). He didn't work for it. He didn't own a successful business. He didn't invent anything. He wasn't a super salesman or marketer. The only thing Abraham did was get up and go where God told him to go (Genesis 12:2); and he believed God and it was accounted to him for righteousness.

Abraham was in covenant with God and God made him very wealthy. He left Egypt very rich after the Pharaoh gave him sheep, oxen, donkeys, camels and servants (Gen. 12:16). Abimelech gave him that and land also. We are the seed of Abraham and God wants to bless us because that's why Jesus shed His blood. He came to redeem us from the curse of lack and poverty and bring us back to our rightful position.

We are the real children of God and joint heirs with Christ. Think about that. God is our father. Anyone who has a rich dad gets two great benefits. One of the benefits is that the father will use his financial strength to help advance the child. The second benefit is that the child can learn everything from the father about how he got his wealth. The child benefits from the wisdom of the father.

We're not to depend on our own abilities or education or contacts to bring us finances. We have access to the wisdom of God, our Heavenly Father. Jesus exchanged our poverty for His wealth.

2 Corinthians 8:9
For you know the grace of our Lord Jesus Christ, that though He was rich, yet for your sakes He became poor, that you through His poverty might become rich.

This is talking about what Jesus did on the cross. The same blood that remitted our sins got rid of lack. We receive financial prosperity the same way we got saved, by faith in the blood. When we apply the blood of Jesus to our finances we can expect the life that is in that blood to drive out death in our finances. Debt is financial death.

Proverbs 22:7
The rich rules over the poor,
And the borrower is servant to the lender.

Debt is a result of the spirit of lack in a person's life. Debt comes from not having enough to live the lifestyle you're trying to live. Many times a person gets in debt because they want something that they can't afford yet. They want it so bad that they're not willing to wait until they grow up into God's prosperity for their lives. The bible tells us that we will prosper in direct relationship to our soul or mind prospering.

3 John 2
Beloved, I pray that you may prosper in all things and be in health, just as your soul prospers.

When a child of God is continuing to live in lack and coming up short every month, it's because they don't have a prosperous soul. It's not that God is holding out on them. Their mind is not renewed to the financial will of God for their life. They need a revelation of what the blood of Jesus did for them financially. Jesus came to give us the abundant life (John 10:10). That abundant life is in His blood because the life of the flesh is in the blood. God has already done everything for you and I to live a superabundant life. That's what the word "abundant" means in John 10:10. It means "way more than enough" or "an overflow".

Jesus became poor on the cross so that you and I could become rich. Yes rich! Rich is not a dirty word for Christians. It's in the bible. We are the seed of Abraham according to Galatians 3:29 and Abraham was extremely rich! We're supposed to be walking in the blessing of Abraham. Jesus shed His precious blood so we could have a life of super-abundance.

I once read about a man who pleaded the blood of Jesus over his paycheck and received a raise. That may sound silly to some people. How can you receive financial increase by just speaking the blood of Jesus over your paycheck? Well, the same way you get your sins remitted when you call upon the name of the Lord and are saved. You can't do it without faith in the blood.

The more revelation you have of what the blood of Jesus did for your material wealth, the more faith you'll have for financial increase when you use the blood. It's obvious this man had faith in the blood's power for provision.

If you will approach God's word with humility, and diligently seek Him for a revelation of His financial plan for your life, you can only come to one conclusion. Jesus blood was shed for you to have a life of abundance; full of health, full of peace, full of joy and full of wealth.

The bible says that it's impossible to please God without faith. It's not because God is hard to get along with. It's not because it's just one of God's "rules" and He's just stubborn about it. It's because you can't *receive* anything from God on this earth without faith. God is only pleased when we receive from Him. Faith is what brings heaven to earth.

Romans 4:16
Therefore it is of faith that it might be according to grace, so that the promise might be sure to all the seed.

We must receive everything from God through faith. If it came any other way, you and I would have to earn it. Faith allows us to receive all that God has for us through His grace. God gives us everything through faith in Jesus because He has chosen to favor us with His grace.

I believe poverty and lack in His children grieves God more than we could imagine. Preachers that teach and preach poverty must really annoy God. If there is any one event in recent history that illustrates the curse of poverty, it's what happened in New Orleans during hurricane Katrina in 2005. Lives were destroyed because of poverty. You may say "Oh no, it was Katrina that destroyed those peoples lives". I beg to differ.

The only thing that kept many of those people trapped in that city was lack of money. Anyone with enough money to get out of town could have avoided all that tragedy. They may have lost some possessions, but they would be alive. They would not have gone through those terrible days, not knowing if they would even survive.

The sad thing is that many of those people were Christians. They had a covenant with God, ratified by the shed blood of Jesus Christ. They had a blood-bought right to live in abundance because Jesus sacrifice gave them that right. In fact, Proverbs 11:10 tells us God's people must prosper in order for a city to do well.

Prov 11:10
When the righteous prosper, the city rejoices;
when the wicked perish, there are shouts of joy.
NIV

The blood of Jesus has given us power to get wealth. Look at Deuteronomy 8:18.

18 "And you shall remember the LORD your God, for it is He who gives you power to get wealth, that He may establish His covenant which He swore to your fathers, as it is this day.

God is talking to Israel here but we have a covenant with the same God. Since God is the same yesterday, today and forever, that would mean He deals with His covenant children the same. Besides, we have a better covenant established on better promises (Hebrews 8:6).

Many believers look at Deuteronomy 8:18 as a *giving* scripture. They see God wanting to give us financial resources to fund the spread of the gospel. They think the "covenant" in this scripture refers only to people who are not saved yet. God wants to establish His covenant with the unsaved and therefore we need money to spread the gospel.

I do believe God wants us wealthy so that there is no shortage to get the gospel out all over the earth. But I believe the covenant He wants to establish is with His covenant people by giving them wealth.

That's what He did for the children of Israel. Now, He wants to show us off. If you're in covenant with someone, you have access to all his resources. That's a basic part of a covenant. If we are God's children and have a blood covenant with Him, we should look the part. We should act the part. God wants the unsaved to look at His children and see that they are well taken care of. They are blessed.

If you tell someone you have a covenant with the creator of heaven and earth, how do you look to them if you're broke, busted and disgusted! That wouldn't make sense to anyone with a brain. How can you claim to be a covenant partner with almighty God and not have access to His resources? No wonder Christianity has been looked down on by so many in the world who have money. It doesn't add up when you tell them how good your God is, but they can see how much you're struggling financially.

But through the blood of Jesus, God has translated us into His kingdom. All the resources of the kingdom belong to us by faith in His blood. Grab hold of your blood bought right to abundance. Plead the blood over everything financial in your life; your debts, your paycheck, your investments. The blood of Jesus is speaking for you in heaven right now. Agree with the blood! You have a right to claim God's best because He provided the best for you through His Son.

9

The Sprinkling of The Blood

Hebrews 11:28
28 By faith he kept the Passover and the sprinkling of blood, lest he who destroyed the firstborn should touch them.

1 Peter 1:1-2
who are chosen 2 according to the foreknowledge of God the Father, by the sanctifying work of the Spirit, that you may obey Jesus Christ and be sprinkled with His blood:
NASB

I have included this chapter as a resource for you to start applying the blood of Jesus to your life. It's not enough to just know about the blood. That knowledge must be applied. That's the definition of wisdom; "skillful application of knowledge".

A picture of this can be found in the story of the original Passover. Moses told the children of Israel that they must kill the lamb and apply the blood to their homes. It wasn't enough just to kill the lamb or to believe that it was possible for that lamb's blood to bring deliverance. The head of every household had to obey Moses' instructions. They had to *apply* the blood to the doorposts of their homes or God would not pass over them and the destroyer would be allowed in their house. That was their faith in *action*.

It's the same with Christians today. We can't just mentally acknowledge Jesus blood shed for us. We must actively apply it to our lives on a daily basis. The blood of the lamb has redeemed us. Christ is our Passover Lamb

(1 Cor. 5:7) and we apply His blood to our lives by faith; speaking faith (see chapter 3 "Why you must have faith in the blood").

The blood of Jesus is in heaven speaking for us (Hebrews 12:24) but we must speak the blood over own lives here on earth. The kingdom of God is in us. We've been raised up together with Christ and are seated in heavenly places with Him (Ephesians 2:6). We are in two places at once. Our bodies are here on earth and our spirits are part of the body of Christ positioned at the right hand of God almighty.

Matthew 16:19 says that God has given us the keys of the kingdom of heaven. Read the Amplified version of this verse. We are to declare on earth what is allowed in heaven. When we say what the blood has already provided for us—healing, protection, peace, prosperity, divine favor—we "loose" or allow those things in our lives and the gates of hell cannot prevail against us.

The following confessions are framed from the word of God and contain applications of the blood of Jesus. Speak them over yourself and your family. Say them several times a day. As you say them, see the blood of Jesus covering your situation and the enemy backing off because of the blood. The destroyer could not penetrate the blood on the night of the first Passover and he cannot penetrate the blood of Jesus when you put it on your house.

I have listed the scripture reference(s) after each confession. It's good to confess these scriptures out loud also. This will build your faith in God's word on the blood.

These are only a few confessions. I believe in quality over quantity. It's not how many different confessions you say. It's whether or not you have faith in them or not. You can run the devil off with one scripture if you have faith in that one scripture. So start building your faith in the blood of Jesus today. By faith keep the Passover (Christ) and the sprinkling of the blood and the destroyer will not touch you!

Fear

"By the blood of Jesus, I am free from fear. Through death, Jesus has released me from the bondage of fear."

Hebrews 2:14-15
14 Inasmuch then as the children have partaken of flesh and blood, He Himself likewise shared in the same, that through death He might destroy him who had the power of death, that is, the devil, 15 and release those who through fear of death were all their lifetime subject to bondage.

"By the blood of Jesus, I'm redeemed from the curse of fear. I'm redeemed from Deuteronomy 28:66. My life does not hang in doubt before me: I fear nothing at all, and have assurance of life. Jesus blood has set me free from fear"

Deuteronomy 28:66
66 Your life shall hang in doubt before you; you shall fear day and night, and have no assurance of life.

"I am a new creature in Christ. I have a new spiritual DNA through the blood of Jesus. I no longer have a spirit of fear, but of power, love and a sound mind."

2 Cor 5:17
17 Therefore, if anyone is in Christ, he is a new creation; old things have passed away; behold, all things have become new.

2 Tim 1:7
7 For God has not given us a spirit of fear, but of power and of love and of a sound mind.

Romans 8:15
15 For you did not receive the spirit of bondage again to fear, but you received the Spirit of adoption by whom we cry out,"Abba, Father."

Healing

"In the name of Jesus, I sprinkle the blood of Jesus on my body. Jesus bore my sins in His body on the tree. I am dead to sin and alive to righteousness. I declare my body healed by the stripes of Jesus."

1 Peter 2:24
24 who Himself bore our sins in His own body on the tree, that we, having died to sins, might live for righteousness—by whose stripes you were healed.

"Christ has redeemed me from the curse of the law. Therefore I'm redeemed from every sickness and every disease in this earth. I declare the life that's in the blood of Jesus drives death and disease out of my body."

Galatians 3:13
13 Christ has redeemed us from the curse of the law, having become a curse for us (for it is written, "Cursed is everyone who hangs on a tree"),

Deuteronomy 28:60-61
60 Moreover He will bring back on you all the diseases of Egypt, of which you were afraid, and they shall cling to you. 61 Also every sickness and every plague, which is not written in this Book of the Law, will the LORD bring upon you until you are destroyed.

"The life of the flesh is in the blood. The life of God is in the blood of Jesus. Jesus gave me abundant life and that life was in His blood. I

have the life of God in me and that life flows throughout my body bringing healing and health."

John 1:4
4 In Him was life, and the life was the light of men.

Romans 8:11
11 But if the Spirit of Him who raised Jesus from the dead dwells in you, He who raised Christ from the dead will also give life to your mortal bodies through His Spirit who dwells in you.

Abundant Life

"By the blood of Jesus I have and enjoy life in abundance, to the full, till it overflows."

John 10:10
10 The thief comes only in order to steal and kill and destroy. I came that they may have and enjoy life, and have it in abundance (to the full, till it overflows).
AMP

"I have victory through the blood of Jesus. The blood has disarmed all principalities and powers ranged against me. Therefore, in the name of Jesus I put the blood of Jesus against you Satan and disarm you from having any power over me."

Col 2:15
15[God] disarmed the principalities and powers that were ranged against us and made a bold display and public example of them, in triumphing over them in Him and in it [the cross].
AMP

"The life of God is in me. The law of the Spirit of life in Christ Jesus has made me free from the law of sin and death. Darkness cannot overtake me because in me is the light that's in the blood of Jesus."

John 1:4-5
4 In Him was life, and the life was the light of men. 5 And the light shines in the darkness, and the darkness did not comprehend it.

Romans 8:2
2 For the law of the Spirit of life in Christ Jesus has made me free from the law of sin and death.

"By the blood of Jesus, I'm free from a rebellious life and I live a pure life, energetic for goodness."

Titus 2:14
14 He offered himself as a sacrifice to free us from a dark, rebellious life into this good, pure life, making us a people he can be proud of, energetic in goodness.
THE MESSAGE

Wealth

"I am rich because the wealth creating blood of Jesus covers me. Jesus exchanged my poverty for His wealth at the cross. Through His grace I have become rich. God gives me power to get wealth because I'm in covenant with Him through the shed blood of Jesus at Calvary."

2 Corinthians 8:9
For you know the grace of our Lord Jesus Christ, that though He was rich, yet for your sakes He became poor, that you through His poverty might become rich.

Deuteronomy 8:18
"And you shall remember the LORD your God, for it is He who gives you power to get wealth, that He may establish His covenant which He swore to your fathers, as it is this day.

"Through the blood of Jesus I have and enjoy life in abundance, to the full, till it overflows. There is no lack in my life."

John 10:10 The thief comes only in order to steal and kill and destroy. I came that they may have and enjoy life, and have it in abundance (to the full, till it overflows).
AMP

"I'm redeemed from the curse of poverty. According to the 28th chapter of Deuteronomy, poverty is under the curse and According to Galatians 3:13, Christ has redeemed me from the curse by His shed blood. Therefore I refuse poverty and lack in my life."

Galatians 3:13
13 Christ has redeemed us from the curse of the law, having become a curse for us (for it is written, "Cursed is everyone who hangs on a tree"),

Deut 28:17
17 You will be cursed with baskets empty of fruit, and with kneading bowls empty of bread.
NLT

Deut 28:38-40
38 "You will plant much but harvest little, for locusts will eat your crops. 39 You will plant vineyards and care for them, but you will not drink the wine or eat the grapes, for worms will destroy the vines. 40 You will grow olive trees throughout your land, but you will never use the olive oil, for the trees will drop the fruit before it is ripe.
NLT

"Abraham was extremely rich in livestock and in silver and in gold. I am in Christ and I'm Abraham's seed and an heir according to the promise. Therefore I am extremely rich. The blessing of Abraham is on my life."

Genesis 13:2
Abram was very rich in livestock, in silver, and in gold.

Galatians 3:29
And if you are Christ's, then you are Abraham's seed, and heirs according to the promise.

Divine Favor

"I'm righteous through the blood of Jesus, therefore God blesses me and surrounds me with a shield of divine favor."

Psalms 5:12
12 For You, O LORD, will bless the righteous;
With favor You will surround him as with a shield.

2 Corinthians 5:21
21 For He made Him who knew no sin to be sin for us, that we might become the righteousness of God in Him.

"Thank you Father God for looking on me with favor, making me fruitful and increasing my productivity, keeping Your covenant with me. That covenant that was ratified by the shed blood of Jesus. I'll still be eating last year's harvest when I'll have to move it out to make room for the new."

Lev 26:9-11 "'I will look on you with favor and make you fruitful and increase your numbers, and I will keep my covenant with you. 10 You will

still be eating last year's harvest when you will have to move it out to make room for the new.
NIV

"Though the blood of Jesus, I have received the abundance of God's favor and the gift of righteousness and I'm reigning as a king in life through Jesus Christ."

Rom 5:17
… those who receive [God's] overflowing grace (unmerited favor) and the free gift of righteousness [putting them into right standing with Himself] reign as kings in life through the one Man Jesus Christ (the Messiah, the Anointed one).
AMP

Applying the Blood of Jesus for Your Salvation

The first application of Jesus' blood you must make is for your own personal salvation. Jesus said "you must be born again" (John 3:7). You must be born of the Spirit of God.

Just as the blood that flows through your veins gives life to your natural body, the blood of Jesus is required to give life to your spirit man.

When you accept Jesus as the substitute for your sin and make Him the Lord of your life, you receive a new spiritual DNA and become a new creation.

2 Corinthians 5:17
17 Therefore, if anyone is in Christ, he is a new creation; old things have passed away; behold, all things have become new.

Romans 10:9 says that "if you confess with your mouth the Lord Jesus and believe in your heart that God has raised Him from the dead, you will be saved". Jesus was raised from the dead by the blood of the everlasting covenant (Heb 13:20). He did it for you and I, so that we could have life in abundance, to the full, till it overflows (John 10:10 Amplified version).

If you would like to become a born-again child of God and receive all of your blood-bought benefits, say this out loud.

"Heavenly Father, I come to You in the name of Jesus. I call on the mighty name of Jesus for my salvation and receive Him as my Lord and Savior. I accept the sacrifice You've already provided for me through

the shedding of Jesus precious blood. I believe in my heart that You raised Jesus from the dead and I have been raised up together with Him.

I believe with my heart that I am now the righteousness of God in Christ and I am saved. Thank you Father for saving me. Thank You Father that I'm no longer dead in trespasses and sins but I've been made alive together with Christ and by grace I'm saved. I am no longer under the authority of darkness but I'm translated into the kingdom of the Son of Your love. I'm redeemed by Your blood!"

Scripture References
Romans 10:9, 10
Ephesians 2:5, 6
Colossians 1:13, 14

That's it. If you said that prayer and believed it, you are saved. You are born again. Don't ever say anything else about your salvation. Regardless of how you feel or look, say what God says about you. And if you do sin, you have 1 John 1:9, *" if we confess our sins, He is faithful and just to forgive us our sins and to cleanse us from all unrighteousness"*.

978-0-595-41486-4
0-595-41486-9

Lightning Source UK Ltd.
Milton Keynes UK
03 December 2009

147027UK00001B/228/A